HENLEY PARKS

RETURN TO LOVE

The Essential Guide On How to Revive Your Relationship, Discover How You Can Rekindle the Flames of Love and Bring Back The Spark and Happiness in Your Relationship

Descrierea CIP a Bibliotecii Naţionale a României
HENLEY PARKS
    RETURN TO LOVE. The Essential Guide On How to Revive Your Relationship, Discover How You Can Rekindle the Flames of Love and Bring Back The Spark and Happiness in Your Relationship / Henley Parks. – Bucharest: Editura My Ebook, 2020
    ISBN

HENLEY PARKS

RETURN TO LOVE

The Essential Guide On How to Revive Your Relationship, Discover How You Can Rekindle the Flames of Love and Bring Back The Spark and Happiness in Your Relationship

My Ebook Publishing House
Bucharest, 2020

Table Of Contents

FOREWORD

It is always said that building relationship is easy but make it sustain and make it last forever is difficult. This is a very tough reality to accept that you always have to compromise some things to make a relationship grow.

Whether these compromises are in your personality, in your life style or in any other thing but these compromises will ensure that you have done something to make your relationship stronger.

Especially when you talk about husband wife relationship then, there are so many important things to know about this relationship which people often ignore and get them in trouble.

Husband wife relationship is not the only relationship which needs your attention to stay intact instead all of your relationships like mother, father, brother, sister, in laws and even friendship also needs certain ingredients which can make your average relationship a very strong one.

In this EBook I will tell you all of those secretes which you can implement in your life and if you have some trouble with any of your present or past relationship you will be able to revive those troubled relationships without any difficulty.

This will take some time to adopt all of these things mentioned in this EBook but with very little but constant effort you will be able to revive all of your relationships successfully. You must have read lots of articles and may be having taken the advice of your lawyer in different relation problems but believe it or not relationships are never solved through those tactics instead such things always make them worse.

There are some basic attitude adjustments and very small life style adjustments that can bring you closer to your relations. Read this EBook carefully and follow whatever is mentioned in it and I am 100 percent sure that you will be able to resolve all kind of problems from your relationships.

Revive Your Relationships

Spark The Flames Of Love All Over With These
Relationship Revival Tools

CHAPTER 1

BASIC NEEDS OF RELATIONSHIPS

Synopsis

There are some basic requirements which are common in almost every relationship and in this chapter I will tell you all of those.

❖ Responsibility from both ends

❖ Take care of your relationships

❖ Enhance communication between your relationships

❖ Give your loved ones their time

The Basics

We all strive for good relationships in all fields of our life because without good and effective relationships it becomes very hard to survive in the society. Good and healthy relationships are also essential for our physical and mental health but we often lack these kinds of healthy and long lasting relationships whther it comes to friends, family or husband wife. You can have troubles with any of your relationship. There has been a great research going on which emphasis on finding the true parameters of a healthy relationship and surprisingly they have come to know some very basic things which almost every one of us knows but we often forget to implement those facts in our daily lives and screw our relationships. Following are some of the basic rules which can create magic for your relationship.

Responsibility from Both Ends

Feeling yourself responsible is very crucial in relationships and no matter which relationship you are talking about but you must feel yourself responsible at one end. Take care of certain things for example if it is relationship with your little sister then, instead of just playing the blame game that she made boyfriend whom you do not like you should take some responsibility and say that if I am wrong then, let it be and listen to your sister whole story carefully and without any biasing make the decision with your full responsibility which is to keep your little sister happy and safe.

Talking rudely and considering yourself always right is not the ways to handle any relationship whether it is relationship with your elder, with your Youngers or with your mates but you need to be polite and proactive about your thoughts.

If you start feeling yourself responsible then, it will allow you to find some mutual agreements which will be beneficial for the both parties. If you are really after flourishing your relationships then, add some responsibility in those relationships and things will start to get better.

Take Care of Your Relationships

Care is another very crucial part of your relationships because no matter which relationship you have but you will always love to have someone caring about you. This is human nature that we always love attention and care. Similar case applies to everyone who is attached to you. Your family, your friends, and your girlfriend everyone is starving for your care and attention. You must have heard that saying that you only get what you give and this saying applies to relationships perfectly. You cannot expect your friends to take care of you if you are not providing them with that care. Similarly your girlfriend will never trust you if you keep checking his phone calls and emails. It's all give and take because nobody in this world is perfect which includes you as well. There are shortcomings in everyone but you need to ignore those shortcomings found in other if you want that they should ignore you. If you started to explore their shortcomings then, it will start a war in which both parties will always be looking for some bad things in each other.

You also need to take care of the emotional bank in your relationship. This is true that whenever you make a relationship then, an emotional bank account is created and your actions, feelings, words, gestures and everything which you do in that relationship adds some emotions in that bank account. If you deposit happy moments, good gestures, caring feeling then, you can withdraw love and care in return but if you start to deposit hate, secrets, rude behavior, ignorance then, it will make things worse and you will not get anything in return but your emotional account will get jammed and you will not be able to withdraw anything.

Enhance Communication between Your Relationships

Communication failure is another thing which causes chaos in relationships because most of the people take communication in a negative perspective and they think that they conveyed their idea, their thoughts and their rules which completes their communication but this is just one half of the communication and you are missing the other half which is listening and understanding the thoughts and ideas of other party. You need to stop thinking that everyone around you also thinks as your do because this is the worst approach which your mind often convinces you to adopt but you need not to adopt it. Even if you need to reject their idea then, first listen to them carefully and then give a logical explanation of your rejection. You need to understand the differences between the both parties. You may be on different grounds while the other one may be on totally different grounds. If you are able to understand and cope with these differences then, you can certainly make that relationship work for you.

Give Your Loved Ones Their Time

Time is also a crucial thing in building relationships because every relationship will need your time. You need to adjust your routine accordingly and nourish all of your relationships with proper timing. Instead of keeping your routine very tight and predictable make it unpredictable sometimes and pay a visit or two without your routine. Escape your work somehow in mid-week and pay a visit to your father. He will be very happy to see you around in middle of the week and will also appreciate your effort that you have prioritized him over your work. Similarly relationships are made stronger when you share ups and downs of life together. If your friend is in trouble then, it is your responsibility to be with him at that time of crises and if you do that then, he will never forget your gestures and will get more attached with you.

If you can implement all of the above things in your life then, it will make all of your relationships better and more solid. These are very common and routine things but in busy routine of our life, we often overlook all of these factors and it creates fuss around our relationships. Keep these things in mind and make your relationships stronger and smoother.

CHAPTER 2

MAKING YOUR HUSBAND-WIFE RELATIONSHIP STRONGER

Synopsis

In this chapter, I will emphasis on relationship of husband and wife and will guide for some things which can make this relationship more concrete.

- ❖ Rules are to be followed
- ❖ Happy housemates
- ❖ Keep romance alive in your relationship
- ❖ Financial predictability

Make It Better

If you are experiencing troubles in your daily routine relationships and tensions and itching in your husband wife relationship then, you must know that there are certain very important things which you need to consider and then implement those things in your life. In the following discussion I am going to tell you about those things.

Rules Are To Be Followed

Every relationship works around a certain set of rules and if you start forgetting about those rules then, things will start to become problematic. We need some rules for our social safety and security similarly, you need some rules to work with your colleagues, your partner and even with your kids. These rules are very important in husband wife relationship and both the parties should lay down these rules with mutual understanding and both should respect those rules. In other words you can say that you need to be very clear with the other person and tell him or her in advance that these are the things which should be never committed in this relationship. Most of the times problem starts when people do not tell each other their differences and the other person keeps guessing the reason of other person's anxiety. For example instead of sitting in car and making different red faces, you should tell your partner that you need to go under or above a certain speed and the problem will be solved and you will face no stress in the end. Similarly, if you are a husband then, you can say that I always need some fresh juice in the fridge because I like to drink it throughout the and this will make the life for both of you lot easier because you both will start to know each other's needs and will start to respect those needs as well.

Happy Housemates

Love is an important element in making the relationship grow but if you start thinking that love is the only thing which can make your relationship grow then, you are mistaken because there are so many other things and especially when you start living under one roof then, there is a certain set of responsibilities on both heads. You need to make yourself a part of that house and start working for its betterment. If you are husband then, you should not be shy to work in your house and help your wife in every day's cores like dusting, cleaning the pool, making breakfast and other similar activities. Similarly if you are a wife then, it becomes your duty to help your husband in releasing the every day's stress. You need to greet him well in the house instead of just watching him and start shouting. When he comes back home after a tiring day at office then, he do not need much more than a coffee and a smiling wife. If he can get that then, it will give him a feeling that his whole day's work is paid and he has worked for a better cause.

Keep Romance Alive In Your Relationship

It is seen that when relationship gets little old then, people start to become predictable in everything. They make a fixed routine of doing everything and even they add romance in that same routine. This is not the right approach because you need to keep romance alive throughout your relationship.

You need to bring an element of surprise in your relationship and break that predictability of your relationship. This is an easy task as you can just escape from your work for one day and come back home in the afternoon and tell your wife that you missed her and you need to spend some time with her alone. Take her to some quiet place and talk about things which you like. This element of surprise is always healthy for relationship and it helps the other partner think that you still care for her. Similarly if you are a wife then, you can go to your husband's office in lunch break with some snacks and tell him that you made these for him. This will give an unexpected pleasure to your husband and he will respect your thoughts and your emotions a lot.

Financial Predictability

According to a research financial instability and disputes of money have been a top reason for divorce and relationship ending. This means that you need to have a sound financial background to have a smooth relationship but money itself is not that much important because people with almost no money have survived in very bad conditions but have not led down their relationships. This is all about responsibility and making your partner to believe that you are trying your best to make things better. Women can stand with you even in toughest situations but they need to know that you are trying hard to make this situation better.

CHAPTER 3

IMPROVING ADOLESCENT

Synopsis

In this chapter, I will tell you about different problems which parents can face during the growth of their kids and will also guide you for the solution.

- ❖ Develop an understanding
- ❖ Social changes
- ❖ Psychological changes
- ❖ Physical maturation
- ❖ Support and affection

Making It Better

Adolescence can be a tough period for both parents as well as their kids because in this period your kids grow physically as well mentally and it becomes difficult for you to come to their level and guide them for the right path. There is another fact that most of the parents neglect their kids in that period of growth because when their kids are growing rapidly and entering in a new age then, parents are more concerned about their own bodies. You need to know that at a time when your teen age kids are entering into adulthood and are ready enter into their practical lives then you need to help them in making big decisions because they accept very strong guidance from you as you have gone through all of that in your age. If you neglect their time then, they will stray in different direction and decisions which they make for themselves will not be very pleasant all the times. There are certain things which you need to know and understand for proper and decent adolescent training of your kids. Following are the key points for you to improve your adolescent approach.

Develop an Understanding

In order to understand and help your teen ager kids, you need to come to their level and understand their teen age world thoroughly. You need to understand that adolescence is a time of transition and change, and if you are able to understand that change properly then, you will be a great help to your kids and this transition and change will occur in almost every aspect of life.

Social Changes

Social changes can sometimes occur from watching friends and your kids will always look at their age group for style, fashion, clothing and other regular things. This sometimes gives you an impression that your kids are not on the right path but you need to understand that these are just some social gestures which are bound to be age and society oriented. You cannot tell you kid that he or she needs to have long hair or short hair because this is one of their very own attribute which they have to adopt according to their surrounding and believe it or not but they know their surrounding better than you. Despite of this social changes and freedom, they will still look to you for moral and behavior values that are a good thing.

Psychological Changes

Psychology of your kids also go through a transition phase and especially because they are going from a dependent stage to an independent stage. They often strive for little more freedom that their parents are willing to offer but this push is just that psychological change which tells them that they have to learn to live at their own at some point of their life and they just want to rehearse that before time.

Physical Maturation

Physical growth is another very important factor which you need to understand as a parent because during adolescence body grows rapidly and this rapid growth allows the child to look in a different way ate him or herself. Their sex glands and other physical attributes also grow very rapidly and sometimes they cannot understand what is going on in their body. This is the time when parents need to guide them properly and tell them that whatever they are feeling is absolutely normal and there is nothing to be afraid of neither it is anything which they should be shy off. This kind of small guidance can make your relationship very pleasant and effective.

Support and Affection

Support and affection are two more important things because kids will always need your support whether that is moral support, some words spoken in the interest of your kid or anything else like that but kids appreciate this kind of support a lot and this gives them lots of confidence to move forward because it gives them a belief that they have someone to back them in their lives. Affection is something which you have to show from your actions. Some parents assume that their kids always know about their love. This is not the right attitude because you need to show your affection whether this is done through your words, a hug or a kiss but you need to make them think that you are always with them and you love them unconditionally.

CHAPTER 4

6 TIPS FOR STRENGTHENING YOUR RELATIONSHIPS

Synopsis

In this chapter I will tell you 6 different and easy to implement tips which you can execute and make all of your relationships better.

- ❖ Always be positive and look for good in yourself first
- ❖ Happiness is unconditional
- ❖ Change yourself first and then expect someone to change
- ❖ Learn to forgive
- ❖ Practice spirituality
- ❖ Raise your expectations and start expecting good

Tips

You must have seen people who are always very contented with their lives and whenever you ask them, they will tell you that they are going very smooth with all of their relationship and there is minimum amount of stress and anxiety in their lives. These people are not from heaven instead they are also human beings like you and me but they just have discovered some better ways of living their lives and these ways are so deeply integrated in their lives that you cannot even notice the difference between your and their approach to life. If you can integrate following 6 things in your life style then, your life will become lot better and lot easier that you have ever imagined.

Always Be Positive and Look For Good In Yourself First

When you start expecting good from other then, you often forget that others are also expecting good form you and if you are not providing them with enough goodness then, you will ultimately get similar things in return. No matter what kind of situation you are in with your relationship but never let the positive edge go and keep trying your best. If you initiate good response then, you will ultimately get to the positive end of the relationship and will be able to make it stronger and healthier while if you tried form your half heart and you kept some things in your heart then, things will go the other way round and you will be left alone without that relationship.

Happiness Is Unconditional

Some people have this habit of associating their happiness with certain personality or certain event but this is not the way to go and your happiness should be unconditional. There are endless things in life which can create happiness for you. You can ignore so many bad things in life and concentrate on so many positives that it will fill your life with happiness.

Change Yourself First and Then Expect Someone To Change

This is natural human instinct that he or she tends to see others changing for them. You have the same nature as you always want to impose yourself and your own rules on others. This is the wrong approach because if you want others to change for you then, you should start this process form you and change yourself fort some of your relationships. This will increase your respect in yes of that relation and he or she will also tend to change accordingly.

Learn To Forgive

Forgiveness is a great virtue as well as it is a very helpful thing in relationships. If you have this small habit of ignoring small mistakes and forgiving people then, it can help you a lot in making your relationships more concrete and strong. Most of the break ups and other family problems arise because today's materialistic life has made us so rigid that we are not ready to give up our ego and forgive anyone. Even I have seen that sometimes the issue is so minor that can be easily forgiven and overlooked but people make a big issue out of a very small deed.

This behavior should be corrected and bring some modesty and forgiveness in your attitude.

Practice Spirituality

Spirituality is something which is a necessary ingredient to make relationships stronger. Spirituality is missing from this world and this is the biggest reason that peace calmness and harmony is also missing from our lives. It is not necessary to believe in certain religion to practice spirituality instead you can practice it through lots of methods for example if you just stop hunting your negative and materialistic desires then, you will get spirituality of one kind and once you achieve that then, you will know that there are so many things which are inter related to those desires and without those desires you can make so many things straight and more realistic in your life.

Raise Your Expectations and Start Expecting the Good

Expectations are also very important because according to the universal law of attraction when you expect something from your deep heart then, everything around you tries to help you to get that particular thing. This is the way to expect that you always need to make your expectations positive and more appropriate in terms of your relationships too.

CHAPTER 5

SECRETS OF STRONG AND HEALTHY FAMILIES

Synopsis

In this chapter I will tell you some basic secrets which you can implement in your family life to make it better and more concrete.

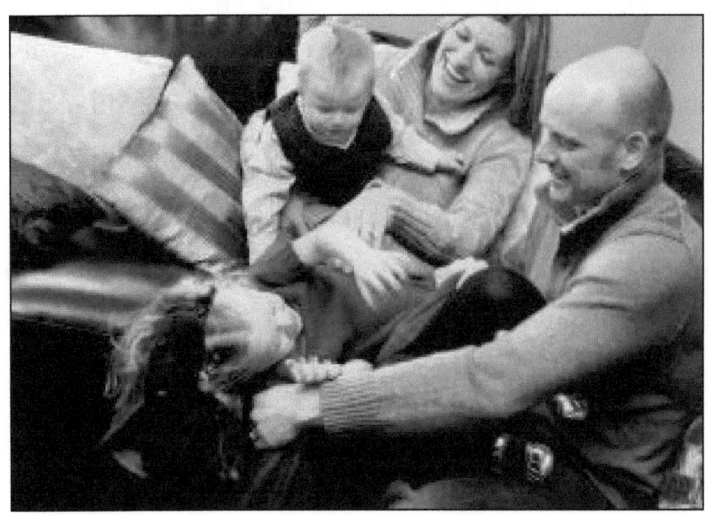

- ❖ Important but difficult task
- ❖ Avoid mistrust and confusion
- ❖ Casual relationships
- ❖ Romantic relationships

Secrets

We are born in a bunch of people who are related to us by blood and these people are called our families. These days you can see lots of chaos around you in society and breaking of family system is one of the greatest reasons behind this chaos. There is no respect in today's society and everyone is unleashed at his or her own. This situation has only one solution and that is to develop your family moral values and tell your family members that you are human beings with certain limitation in society and you are born to have some responsibilities which you have to take whether you like them or not. There are certain limitations in family system and family system is known from those limitations. If there are no rules and limitations in your family system and everyone is free to do whatever they want then, you will suffer from some uncertain and unpleasant effects of this freedom. There are still families present in this society which are very precise about their family system and they are running a very successful family system. Secrets of family system are as follows.

Important but Difficult Task

You need to understand that building healthy relationship with your family is difficult but it is also very important at the same time. There are different people in your family which can be your siblings, your parents, your children or even your grand parnets but it is required that you should talk to everyone at his or her own level. If you are talking to your kid then, you need to be a kid mentally to understand your kid's behavior. If you keep imposing your thoughts without knowing their response then, it will make things worse.

Family system runs on mutual understanding and respect. If you can respect and understand each other then, everything will go smooth but problems start when you start playing that old blame game and start blaming each other for different things.

Avoid Mistrust and Confusion

Mistrust and confusion are like fire for family relationships because when trust is damaged between two souls then, they cannot understand each other. Best way to eliminate all kinds of mistrust and confusion, you need to make sure that communication is fluent and there are no secrets present between different family members. When you start sharing your problems and even your good things with each other then, things will get real smooth. Some people say that they have come to an end of relationship but believe it or not but there is no end to any relationships and especially when you talk about blood relationships like brother, father sister and mother. These relationships are made to stay forever and with very small care and support, you can always make these relationships better and stronger. It is never too late for you to start the healing process for your relationships and you can always find some ways to educate the other party but first you need to make yourself modest, caring and forgiving then, you can expect similar things in return.

Casual Relationships

Casual relationships are those which have no blood relation involved and they are made by just regular and routine acquaintance. For example few colleagues of your office can be in casual relationship with you and sometimes these relationships can be turned into full time relationships. It is necessary that you should keep a certain level of respect and trust in every relationship that you have whether that is a casual relationship or a formal blood relationship but without respect and trust you cannot run any relationship.

Romantic Relationships

Romantic relationships are totally different kinds of relationships which you encounter in your life. Sometimes it can happen that you get in love with someone whom you know from childhood or school time but these days this is not the case because world has gone towards more materialistic environment and people tend to choose their soul mates after researching well behind his or her back and making sure that he or she has a safe future ahead. This is also not a very good act as you need to go with your heart in these matters and avoid researching too much.

CHAPTER 6

THINGS TO AVOID BREAK UPS

Synopsis

There are certain precautions and similar other things which you can do and avoid any break up and I will tell you all such things in this chapter.

❖ Understand each other's family patterns

❖ Timing is also crucial

❖ Emotional support is also important from both ends

❖ Agree to disagree is the policy to adopt

❖ Clarify yourself and then listen carefully

❖ Discuss one thing at a time

The Errors

Disagreements can happen in any relationship but if you can handle these disagreements properly then, they can help you to even strengthen your relationship. It is impossible that you cannot have any anxiety, trouble, disagreement or any similar thing in your relation but there are tactics which can help you in reducing the threat of breaking up your relationship completely. First of all you need to prepare yourself and have a strong intent of solving all the problems.

Understand Each Other's Family Patterns

If you are having problems with your hubby or your wife in very start of your relationship then, you need to have a close look at the family patterns. Analyze both family patterns carefully and think about the differences which are present in those families. Your hubby may be groomed and trained in a different atmosphere while you are expecting something totally different from him. You need to make slight adjustments. This applies to both partners and you can make things better with some mutual compromises and understandings.

Timing Is Also Crucial

If you happen to face some serious problem in your relationship then you should look to give each other sometime. Sometime it is better to be a part for some time and think about each other in a quiet place. It leads to more confrontation if you start looking for a solution right after the problematic situation. If you give each other some time to settle in then, both of you will analyze the situation more deeply and will conclude in the end that it is better to patch up again because the core issue will be found dead and you will be itching to see each other again.

Emotional Support Is Also Important From Both Ends

Emotional support means that you need to give some space to your partner and start accepting the differences that you have with your partner. He or she may become willing to let some of their things go because of your good supportive role.

Agree To Disagree Is the Policy To Adopt

If you are really into saving your relationship then, you need to adopt a simple plan and that is to agree that you can disagree on certain things. This is little hard to understand but once you cope with this policy then, thing will go real simple and even the most impossible looking things will be solved in few minutes. There are few things which you can never overcome and there will be certain differences which you can never avoid. There is only one way to avoid these differences and that is to come into a mutual agreement that both of you will not do certain things which are unacceptable for the other partner.

Clarify Yourself and Then Listen Carefully

This is another thing which most of the couples miss that both of the partners do not tend to listen. They always want that they are to speak in order to clear things. This is good but you should have some self-control and allow the other person to speak and allow you to listen carefully and positively. Adopt all the positive things that you can adopt from his or her point of view and then convey your point of view accordingly. This again involves some mutual understanding and respect because without that both of you will not be able to hear each other out and the problem will stay intact.

Discuss One Thing at A Time

If you ever find yourself in confrontation then, try to discuss only one thing at a time. It is often seen that whenever people get angry then, they start talking about past incidences which makes things even worse and instead of reaching to a solution it creates more fuss and chaos among relationship. You need to make sure that whenever you enter into a discussion to make things better then, try to remain on the most present issue and do not stray here and there and do not start any blame game.

Keep these things in mind and I am sure that you will be able to resolve your problems properly and without any further issues, your relationship will run smoothly.

WRAPPING UP

In the above EBook I have tried to tell you all the important secrets which could help you in making your relationships stronger and healthier. If you have noticed in the whole discussion that I have emphasized on one thing more and that is mutual respect and understanding.

This is most important aspect of any relationship whether you talk about husband wife or parent kids but trust, mutual respect and understanding is the core things which you need to develop in these relationships.

If you keep all of the above things in mind then, you will notice a very pleasant change in your daily life because almost all of your relationships will get better and healthier.

You should also know that less stress and anxiety is also useful for a better health. You will feel lot better when you are not tensed from your family matters.

When you know that you have people who love you and care for you then, it will also boost your career and you will be able to progress more. You can say that if you are able to run a good family then, it will help you to make your whole life better.

You will be able to concentrate on your job and on your work more and you will get results from your work. Relationship building is also a part of your personal productivity and if you are able to understand the sensitivity and demands of personal relationships then, you will be able to adopt that understanding in your professional relations too.

Things that I have mentioned in this EBook are not very hard things to learn or adopt instead these are very routine things and gestures but we all forget to execute them properly.

This EBook is just a reminder that you need to do certain things to keep your relationships alive. So I hope you have enjoyed reading the EBook and the information you found will be helpful and will make your life better.

9 786069 836811

Printed by Libri Plureos GmbH in Hamburg, Germany